CSU Poetry Series XIX

Other books by Roger Mitchell:

Letters from Siberia and Other Poems (1971)

Moving (1976)

Roger Mitchell

A CLEAR SPACE ON A COLD DAY

Cleveland State University Poetry Center

ACKNOWLEDGMENTS

I would like to thank the editors of the following journals where some of these poems first appeared.

Amicus Journal: "Of William Stillman (1828-1901)"
The Chowder Review: "A Dream, With Robert Bly," "Upright and Fallen"
Cream City Review: "For the Children at U.S. Grant School, Sheboygan, Wisconsin"
Indiana Review: "History of the Wind"
Indiana Writes: "Relations"
Mickle Street Review: "To Walt Whitman on America's Birthday"
The Minnesota Review: "Some Thing," "Who Needs a Bicycle"
The New Review (England): "Seeing England," " Homage to Beatrix Potter"
North American Review: "All Hallow's Eve," "Variations"
Omens (England): "A Clear Space," "Mamoo's Death"
Other Poetry (England): "Here Comes History," "Visiting Country Graves With My Daughters"
Pennsylvania Review: "The Two Secretaries"
Ploughshares: "The Life I am Living," "School Dream," "The Story of the White Cup"
Poetry: "Cinderella"
Poetry Northwest: "The Choice," "Now"
Redbook: "For the Children at U.S. Grant School, Sheboygan, Wisconsin"; reprinted from *Cream City Review*
River City Review: "The Little Table," "Keene Valley, Late Fall, Starset," "In the Howard Johnson's in Hammond"
Three Rivers Poetry Journal: "The Feel of Vacancy"
Tracks: "Roots"
Voices (England): "Start"
Windless Orchard: "Starting to Starve"

I would like to thank Ragdale artists' colony where, during several residencies, a number of these poems were written.

The Raintree Press of Bloomington, Indiana published a slightly different version of "Homage to Beatrix Potter" as a pamphlet in 1978. The poem also appeared in the P.E.N. anthology, *New Poems 1977-78*, ed. Gavin Ewart (London, 1978).

ISBN 0-914946-65-X

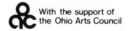 With the support of the Ohio Arts Council

CONTENTS

Variations   11

Homage to Beatrix Potter   13

The Life I am Living   15

To My Sister Who Remembers the Day She Was Born   17

Edges   18

Roots   21

Uneven Light   22

Here Comes History   24

To Walt Whitman on America's Birthday   25

All Hallow's Eve   27

School Dream   30

A Dream, With Robert Bly   32

Pehr Kalm and Lars Yungstroem: Songs and Dances   34

Cinderella   39

The Neighbor   42

A Man   43

Start   44

The Feel of Vacancy   45

Letter to Milwaukee   46

Now   52

The Little Table   53

Relations   54

In the Howard Johnson's in Hammond   56

Who Needs a Bicycle   57

The Choice   58

Upright and Fallen   60

A Clear Space   61

For the Children at U.S. Grant School, Sheboygan, Wisconsin   63

Of William Stillman (1828-1901)   64

The Two Secretaries   67

Mamoo's Death   69

Seeing England   70

Some Thing   72

Starting to Starve   73

The Story of the White Cup   75

Visiting Country Graves with My Daughters   76

Keene Valley, Late Fall, Starset   77

The Incident of the Water   78

The History of the Wind   79

For my mother and father
late thanks

A CLEAR SPACE ON A COLD DAY

VARIATIONS

I

I come back carrying a past
that happened here, but not to me,
and not to any of those like me
who borrowed a piece of the air here,
and when they left, left building dreams
of leaving, and of coming back.

I've wanted to come back smiling,
full of teeth. I've wanted to undo
the frightened boy I knew then,
his foolish cruelties and hate.
I've wanted what I've wanted so,
I hear faint cheering in my dreams.

A boy remembers always what
he'd rather not. A boy spends years
saying the thing he should have said,
but didn't, to the girl who turned
and left him standing in a lot.
She leaves him standing in a lot,

and after twenty years or so,
he gets it right, the boy, standing
in the empty lot in the head
of the grown man, stammering toward
faint light, blowing out the dark.

II

OK, there was no boy standing
in an empty lot. I saw it
in a movie, a bad B flick

in a small town where the popcorn
stank of rancid fat. And the girl,
she was the biggest lie of all.

All right, there was a girl. Her name
was Phoebe. I forget her name.
The bit about the B movie
I made up. It seemed the right place
to learn a bad habit you can't
ever seem to break your mind of.

I was young, though. Do you buy that?
And I stayed young, for a long time.
I married the girl. Jane, I think.
We ate popcorn for seven years,
and watched a bland double feature
that kept on ending till the end.

OK, I give up. I surrender.
Nothing remotely resembling
anything I've said ever was.
I came into the world naked
and alone. After that, things blur.
I fall into a ditch of facts.

HOMAGE TO BEATRIX POTTER

I

I do not know a lot about Beatrix Potter,
but if she were my daughter,
I would tell her not to bother, so much,
about good behavior.

I would wonder what I had done to her
and under what pretext
to have been turned into a Macgregor
for her Peter to anger.

And in a garden, over an issue like property.
And in the company of imploring
but otherwise quite useless sparrows.
Life was difficult in the nineteenth century.

But I don't think mothers, even then,
sent their sons to the usual slaughter
with a chuck under the chin
and a wry word about potted father.

And then went out to buy five currant buns,
including one for their errant son,
who might or might not, according to the whim
of dread, come home again.

I think of the mouse with her mouth full of pea
who stopped to gag something kind
but incomprehensible, and the cat
who twitched at the bright orange fish in the pond.

And the hob-nailed boot that kicked
through the potted plants, and the raised rake,

and the tiny rage at the little rabbit
whose only habit was eating.

I wonder if minding mother would ever matter
in a world of Macgregors, and others,
who like to see some things grow,
but not others.

II

I am the father of Peter Rabbit.
I was eaten by Mr. and Mrs. Macgregor on Sunday
after being skinned in the tool shed,
boned in the kitchen,
and boiled for several hours in a metal pot.
Mr. Macgregor said I was good.
Mrs. Macgregor wasn't sure,
thought I was a bit stringy in places.
I was caught in the French beans,
a rake point driven through my skull.
I lived to be an example to my son.

III

It was the drawings I remember most,
the careful cabbages and a radish
that Peter seemed to pick his teeth with,
the tiny slipper in the dirt, and always
everything about to melt into the page
like snow fallen on clear water, two versions
of the same thing merging, a bright inhuman
whiteness, a small world paling into it,
like animals pretending to be people,
an invisible barrier disappearing,
an unimaginable brotherhood
of living things, as a book stands between
nothing and the person reading it.

THE LIFE I AM LIVING

> *It is a wild, rank place, and there is no
> flattery in it.*
>
> — *Thoreau*

Walking home alone at night,
I see myself as always walking
home alone at night. The wind
walks a cloud across the sky
on a light leash. The moon trembles.
A light goes on somewhere across
a street or yard. I am going
home, the place I left in haste
an hour ago. I couldn't wait
to leave. I was home alone,
and everything was home alone,
the windows, the plates, the things I knew.
The things I knew were there, always,
so I went out and the warm spring
evening that lay between the room
I went to and the house I left
put its arm across my shoulder.
There, it said, smiling. There, there.
Spring would not be unkind,
though I had heard it said, often.
I heard voices, mothers calling
into the dusk, children, muffled,
calling back. They would go home,
this time, and maybe the next,
but they were crouched next to the bush,
whispering: Wait, wait for me here.
I would go home, too, though to what,
I was not sure. Maybe the plates
or the spoons or the steep stairs.
But first I would walk through the trees

to a windowless room high on a hill,
high as the trees, which look that way
because branches, they say,
must not touch one another.
The wind thinks otherwise.
I think otherwise, too. I think
this is not my life, this mulling.
This is not me, not what I meant
when I said it is a wild, rank place.
I look in the lighted windows.
I listen to the sparkling gab
everywhere, the chatter and drone.
I turn it down like a radio
late at night. I keep it by me.
That is me talking of stars.
That is me taking the world by the hand
and leaving. I shall sit by the sea
and read. I shall look in the book
as I would a window, passed at dusk
hoping to find there the life,
the one I am living.

TO MY SISTER WHO REMEMBERS
THE DAY SHE WAS BORN

There was no woman
walking along with a handbag
in the snow, for me, no
brief scene out the window. There was,
as I remember, an immense—
there is no way to say how much—
silence gathered together, whole
armies of stillness, standing there
at ease for my arrival.

It was a sobering affair
to come from nowhere, and not be
anyplace I could remember
longer than my eyes blinked. And,
to be stuck there till, like a slow
leak in a pipe, life
began happening.

                A dull wall, first,
and stairs down into darkness. Then,
light. As though through a slight curtain
or lace. That was probably you,
home from the outer void,
weighted down already with thought.

Like a woman walking along.
Like a woman walking along
the edge of the earth. Which was then,
and is still, just out the window,
just over there, where the snow is.

EDGES

I

For months I have walked this rocky coast,
building my fires in windless cracks,
snaring my birds from the air, fish
from the gray sea. One net for all,
flashing into the element.

I carry my wife inside me.
I bear my children in the wave's hiss.
I swim with the porpoises, naked
and shining, my hair close to me.
The whale sings me his long song.

On land I am flaky. Bits of me
break against stone. The wind looks after
my loosening hair. This falling
apart is my daily miracle.
Night is alive in another place.

II

I am never far from edges.
Here, the land pushes into the sea
and up, as always, into the air.
The white eyes of the sea open
and close like stars everywhere.

I sleep on my arm, rise with it
bloodless, dragging against me, hold
it under the fire to bring it back.

I am not alone. Everything
speaks. Each wave is a tongue. Each stone
is a language rolled into one.

The weeds are dialects of wind
and water.

I will go back some day. Winter
is hard in these caves. The sand stings.
Summer is better, though barely.
I lie on the low rocks where land
and sea come close to each other.

III
This is the time before time.
The waves are one continuous
roar, the wind a single breath, birds
the feathers of the one body.
Light is a version of sight, the heart stone.

This is the sea without stop,
the rolling thorn that grows to itself.
This is the sky holding itself
in its cloudless arms.
This is.

IV
I lie on the hot sand for hours,
my head on the dune grass. It is dark.
Down on the beach there is dancing,
shadows staggering among flames.

The sea makes silence like a noise.
It never stops. The dancers fall,
exhausted, laughing. They think they are drunk.

They smell of meat, salty and burnt.
Even now, they know what they want.
It lies on them sleeping like dew.

The fire falls, at last, like shadow.
Into itself.
The hiss whose silence is its voice
licks us into darkness.

V

The whales have drifted away,
having seen. The wind sucks at my ears.
The sea, too, looks at me sideways,
wrinkling away, through its single squint.
It is time to go back.

The sky's eye rolls in its juices,
milky, looking for its own pupil,
looking for the other eye, lost,
on the far side of its head,
the eye that can see for itself.

ROOTS

It is not, he said to my question
about where we were to sleep while
pouring me a half of bitter,
it is not, though this was my place,
not his, who only lived here, it

is not, where people take other
people into their homes, for rest,
no, not, ever, though once I said
it must have been exactly that
sort of place. It is not, he said.

I went up into the church and
found nothing in my disbelief
but a cozy plaque from Massa-
chusetts, which, too, I hear is now
that sort of place. Where I was born.

UNEVEN LIGHT

I

Four Amish, one man and three women,
enter the Greyhound depot in Columbus, Ohio
at three in the morning.

                They sit apart.

II

Outside, the street gives back a watery,
uneven light.

          After ten minutes of being stared at,
one of the women blossoms into a girl.
She spins on one foot, throws out an arm,
neither motion dislodging her bonnet board.

III

Every dream I have hugged to myself comes back to me,
every dream I have held down to the floor
as it went berserk, murmuring, my knee on its neck.

IV

My mother telling me at age twelve —
had she told me before? — about Santa Claus,
of her dismantling, at the last possible moment,
the last hope of living in a world of pure thought.

V

And my father, the same year, telling me
I was too old now to kiss him goodnight.
I went up to bed and never gave it a thought.
I went upstairs and put it away so carefully
even the wreckers couldn't find it
when they came looking for it thirty years later.
"Goodnight, Dad," I said. Though I see now
how he must have waited for weeks, maybe months,

phrasing it one way, phrasing it another,
the secret weeping in his bloodstream,
like the death of his father when he was twelve
stirring, sliding a few of its fine, sharp grains
downstream.

VI

Where I sit resting from broken sleep
in a strange town, in a plastic chair,
in a depot locked against drifters and drunks,
on the way to visit children I still call
mine.
Watching these Amish, sitting apart.

HERE COMES HISTORY

Here comes history, everything blinking
and flashing, insisting that it can sit
on the horn all day, drive down the wrong side
of any issue it likes, knock the cart
full of carefully piled oranges into the street,
scattering the good gray people of the town
as though we were so much hen dust.
Where is the preacher, the doctor, the good
grim killer we hired to harbor the law?
Is he the one at the wheel, or is he
the one lashed to the stretcher in back,
writhing and dying before he arrives?

TO WALT WHITMAN ON AMERICA'S BIRTHDAY

Walt Whitman has just walked into the room,
and for a moment,
though everyone is looking at him,
no one goes forward to greet him.

It is Walt Whitman, after all,
and what could we possibly say to him
or he to us
that we wouldn't find embarrassing in the morning.

Luckily, someone rescues us from the silence,
someone I know vaguely,
was introduced to once at a function much like this one,
have said hello to in the elevator once or twice
but who works in another department
and so will become someone I greet
less and less over the years
until I do not recognize him at all
and he returns to being someone
I never met.

This person, this someone,
whose name even now escapes me,
asks Mr. Whitman if he would like a glass of sherry.
It is that kind of function.
A waiter in a white coat
who is also a graduate student in economics
appears with a glass of sherry.
Walt Whitman is too stunned to say thank you.
He drinks instead,
looking into the glass.

The person, the same person,
asks several questions.

He wishes to put everyone at ease.
Walt Whitman is already at ease.
He does not hear the questions.
He drinks his sherry, rather quickly,
puts the empty glass in his coat pocket
and leaves.

When he is gone, out of earshot,
we all have a good laugh
at that one.

ALL HALLOWS EVE

and the wind
out walking, out
looking for a bush
to thrash,
out walking all night long
along gutters,
kicking leaves back
across raked grass,
flinging some rain down
hard.

Thirteen years ago,
in a graveyard outside Cracow,
every tombstone soaked
at dusk
in candle light,
the living moving there
in shrouds of flesh.

The children come
with scrawled faces,
pretending to be
what they are,
robber and tiger,
monster and cold blue star.
They thank me
for what they get
by threat,
then run ragged
into the dark.

To Mommy's waiting car
often, but often

on to the next
door bang and gripped soap,
hoping for one
genuine rejection,
somebody caught
thoughtless.

Deep in a year
undistinguished
and indistinguishable
from those
around it,
the wind continues
its nervous
rustle, its nosing
among rubbish
for something to lift.

I, who would cheerfully
be spirited
off,
were the wind to blow
in the right direction,
know that it won't
this year, but go
out anyway
into a neighborhood darkened
by fear and the weather,
where the only light
is the glow
of streetlamp
and gutted pumpkin,
and throw myself like a dishrag
into a sink
full of dirty dishes.
Damn it, I say

to the parked car.
And damn it,
I say to the bush.
And when the cloud
spits in my eye,
damn it, I say
again.

SCHOOL DREAM

I had gone back to the old brown rambling school
with its ancient test tubes, where I wanted to speak
and the person I wanted to speak with was never there
or had just stepped out. They knew me there, or it seemed that way,
though there were girls there now. One of them said hello,
and she and her friends clustered around me, laughing.
I did not feel as old as I was, as the teachers
who occasionally threw their older and knowing eye
like a pall across my suit. It was not new, I admit,
but it was clean. I needed a room, an inexpensive room
to write my book in. I needed a little space,
and the food didn't have to be wonderful,
and if in a way it could be like a place I had known,
a place where they had been paid to believe in me,
if it could be like that hopeful moment when I was poised
before the cruel errors that would make me the dreamer
surrounding himself with beautiful knowing older girls
who thought he was something, or with the long corridors
and dark panelling of the private school that allowed him
to be important and smart and play football
to everyone's amazement, he was so skinny and afraid,
if it could be like that for a while, two or three months,
I might write the book I wanted to write,
as soon as I could remember what it was about.
But I could remember what it was about later
when I had the room and the bed and the small table
in the corner and the lamp and the meals brought to me,
which needn't be anything fancy, and the woods
to walk in and the occasional girl smiling at me
and the teachers who knew more than they told,
keeping their distance, letting this happen because
they knew what it was and knew that someday
they would need to go back to an old rambling past
that had never happened and were secretly cheering

for themselves as they drudged past with their wisdom
and folders, sagged from having been held too long
and rearranged and written everywhere into the margins.
It was the teachers I was afraid of, it was the teachers
who knew too much, more than they wanted to know,
it was the teachers who bore the tell-tale marks,
the tiny scars that no one sees, who had been good at hiding,
and cheering us on at the edge of the field or the end
of the corridor under the light marked "Exit."
They were the dreaming adults we swore we wouldn't become,
who kept us away from home and the world and ourselves.

A DREAM, WITH ROBERT BLY

In my dream the solemn Robert Bly
has been reading his twelve-day poem
on the death of James Wright,
a poem in which death was entirely unmasked
for the first time, in which death ceased
being mysterious, in which
it was no longer a mantel of darkness,
or the third who is always walking beside us,
or the caretaker of a valley of shadows, or
a man with an axe hiding in the bushes.
Nor did it sit innocently in the redbud tree
sticking out its hundred green heart-shaped tongues
and licking us like lollipops as we passed
beneath, giving us the famous kiss
of which we have all no doubt heard plenty from birth,
no.
And when suddenly it became time to wake,
the solemn Robert Bly looked up
from his twelve-day inventory of death' s disguises
and catalogue of weighted robes, convinced
that his friend, James Wright, had slipped past them all
as he was flattering them, as they were standing
in line waiting to be praised in that oily room
that smells only a little and only like an old refrigerator
that has trouble doing its job in the heat of summer,
only a little like that secret rot
which cannot be gotten at no matter how many times
a day you defrost it,
and when James Wright was safely gone,
Robert Bly, in my dream, began to tell us joyfully,
as though we were children, as though he, too, were one,
about the tiny "fack-appy."
We hadn't the slightest idea what it was, the "fack-appy,"

but the tears came down his face
as he told us about it, or, rather,
as he repeated its name in a delighted way.
And that made us forget death
and the twelve-day cramp in our backsides,
and we woke up sweating (or I did)
to the tune of the early morning rush hour traffic,
waving goodbye and saying in the almost empty room,
"fack-appy."

PEHR KALM AND LARS YUNGSTROEM: SONGS AND DANCES

(Pehr Kalm was a botanist and Professor of "Oeconomy" at the University of Abo, Sweden. He was sent by the Swedish Academy to the New World to gather information and seeds to help diversify a limited Swedish agriculture. He was allowed an assistant, Lars Yungstroem, whom he describes as "a gardener well skilled in the knowledge of plants and mechanics, who had at the same time a good hand for drawing." They left Uppsala in October, 1747, spent a few months in England, and then came to the English colonies of North America. What follows is based on their journey in 1749 from the English to the French colonies, from Albany through Lake Champlain to Montreal. They were away from Sweden for several years.)

"Meeting Trees"

We met continually with trees
fallen down. We also met them
upright. We met with trees aslant,
as well, trees half way down, or more.
Though sometimes less. These,
though neither up nor down,
we also met continually.
                    In Sweden, trees
are not like this. We meet, of course,
but less continually.

"Lying Awake at Night"

The air was calm and no leaf stirred.
I lay there listening, the air
calm, the leaves above me stilled.
I had never heard so little
or so much.
        Then, the sudden crack,
the swish of tearing leaves, a thump.
Like the shutting of a door
in a distant entryway.
Like a door shut for the last time.

"The Effluvia"

The effluvia toward evening
were strongest near the river banks,
and though we poled along them, looking,
lifting the heads of strange vetches,
fescues, ferns and flowered vines,
parting the thick vegetation
with a stick, sniffing the least leaf,
we never found what caused them.
We knew what caused that other smell:
the shy, sly, gristly musk rat.

"Hymn to Lars Yungstroem, His Assistant"

Handy with axes, mechanics,
a good hand at drafting, a cook
who can conjure a meal out of
musk rat, a man who can lift,
who can sit, who can smoke a pipe.
Who can tell by feeling the leaf
what the plant is, by the plant
the depth of the root, by the root
the state of the dirt, the nature
of nature.
   Who's Swedish, to boot,
and who knows what heat and the snakes
are, and are plotting. And who smiles.

"Lars' Song of the Beaver"

The beaver bites the tree off neat.
He does it with his teeth.
He builds a dam, says here I am,
you'll find me underneath.

I like the beaver, I like his tail.
It makes a big whack.
The water combs his hair out smooth.
I'd like to take one back.

In Sweden are no beavers.
In Sweden are no dams.
All we have in Sweden is
rutabagas.

"Song of the Captured Boy"

The boy in breeches, shirt and cap
is suddenly a man.
One wonders if, at nine years old,
he'll make an Indian.

His father's head sits on a pole.
There is not much to say.
They have honored their killed brother.
It is their way.

"Lars' Song to the Huron Maiden"

O lovely Huron maiden,
you make me think of Sweden,
your skin
the color of the rutabaga.

"He Writes His Monarch on a Delicate Subject"

As I do not know Huron well,
and, as there is no sign, or none
I could quite bring myself to make,
for the venereal disease,
thinking all the while, Your Highness,
of Sweden and of your high charge,
I regret the secret of the cure,
the root or blossom, remains so.
There were certain smirks among the braves,

as I was broaching the subject,
quite disconcerting, as well as
odd gutteral hoots and low grunts,
which I did not enquire into.
That night, one of their women, flushed,
came to me, but you may be sure
that neither I nor Lars (though not
without reminding Lars of his mother,
twice) has stained the Swedish nation.

"Now and Then"

Now and then a little river
falls. Only now and then. The sound
of water falling is the sound
I heard at birth. I heard it then,
and now, along the lake, little
rivulets of water rattle.
I'm not sure where I am. My book
is packed away, my quill is dull,
and the boat drifts.
                    Look, a fish.
Lars has hooked us dinner. Clever Lars.

CINDERELLA

I

When they found her prostrate in the garden,
talking to a beetle, they locked her in the loft.

There it was spiders. For them, she danced
and made strange noises in her throat.

Nothing could shame her. Tied to the hog trough,
she wallowed in mud and warm moonlight.

At dawn, a sow lay sleeping against her.
She hugged a tree, and they took her clothes away.

She tried to nurse a calf, so they killed it.
And then wiped their hands on her naked breasts.

She would leave all this someday. But for now
she kept to the barn, mooing in the stillness.

II

When she left, she put a tear in a sack
and left it by the back door. It was dawn.

The frog in her palm collected itself
and leapt over the gate.

She would leap like that if she had to.
She would be the fox if the dogs came near.

She followed the ant and the low shrub,
and carried a knife now to bite with.

III

The sisters, naturally, were beautiful.
And, naturally, they were described otherwise.

She knocked on the back door, twice, begging for food.
They stared at her caked thighs, her ropey hair.

One of them threw her a shoe, the other
a cinder, and then watched as she choked them down.

They smiled their smiles in the right places,
but behind the barn they took cats apart.

The boys in the village, though, hung out their tongues
and dreamt. And some of them wept, and some cursed.

She was a broom dressed as a shawl, crouching.
Into her life crept nothing, breathing.

IV

He was not a prince. He was not even rich.
He was a woodcutter, and he drank.

There was no ball, there was no slipper,
and the clock had not yet been invented.

Someone else would think of these things:
the princes and the glass-like elegance,

the indoor bliss and the irreversible
severance from everything living,

the impossible splendor,
life in an up-thrust, thick-moated tower.

She wept at the woodcutter's death,
but dug the grave herself, the same day.

She never went back. She didn't need to.
Birds flittered over the new grass, the moles hummed.

THE NEIGHBOR

I am afraid to watch him too long.
I am afraid he will do something too human.

As it is, he sits on his step,
holding a small package on his arm.

I have no idea what's inside it,
the bag wrinkled everywhere like a new child.

He does not bring his cigaret up to his mouth.
He goes down to it, stooping and affectionate.

A MAN

A man with uncombed hair, hair that veers
in several ways at once, as a flight of birds
at the last moment swerves from the tree
in which it meant to land, a man
with his shirt pulled out on one side, a man
half there, the other half somewhere we can't see,
yet see that we can't see, like Oslo
on a map, like the inside of the wind,
a man in a swaggering, stupefied limp,
belligerent, a short-legged stagger,
as though the earth were at sea and the stars
with it, a man, the length of the locked depot,
afloat in a loveless glare, a man,
all night, in Columbus, Ohio.

START

Not knowing whether I have pre-
pared myself sufficiently, no
longer caring, concerned only,
as the wave of my fortieth
year breaks over me, that I try—

what, I am not sure, but the thing
that I have dreamt of, and dreaming,
long longed to bring forth, tumbling
in its harness, voluminous
in its rude grace, and sufficient,

that that energy, neither mine
nor yours, but ours, abide with us,
presumptuous and insistent,
the deliberate gaiety
of the nail driven, and driving, home.

THE FEEL OF VACANCY

I want to say that the wind is blowing
and that behind this wind is another
less visible than the first but also blowing
and that the blowing of this second wind
has about it all the feel of vacancy
and that it is very strong so strong
that there is a kind of humming of the blood
which attends it as an attendant would attend
and that though strong it is also gentle
and that when it gets through blowing
or at a certain moment in its blowing
which no one can predict with certainty
the grass will all be leaning and the trees
even the houses will have acquired a slant
all in the same direction and the wind
the air space itself will not stop but keep blowing
in memory of the most immediate
and instant incipience of its motion.

LETTER TO MILWAUKEE

As I lay last night under the knife
of your hot breath, that blade now rusted,
garbage burning in the outer suburbs,
as I lay there drawing breath and comparisons
under the weak ether of the window slit,
and the carbon depositing under my tongue,
and me being new to Milwaukee and all,
I thought of writing you.

You have a mind of dirt, the wisdom
to lie there and be walked on, to be prodded,
to be pushed anywhere except out of sight.
The black tree reaches up out of you
like a hand slipping out of sight
from the middle of a bare block under the Juneau Towers,
the glint of old sidewalks just under the stubble
and bottom steps crumbled like saved cake.

The unfinished ramp stops
at the boarded fourth-story windows
of an abandoned factory,
a frozen ejection of cement.
Dotted lines dump into the lake
beyond fresh excavations,
forums of threaded columns
rising from buried riverbanks.
Slums in the arms of interchanges,
stone octopuses wrestle the sky.

The young executives in their sideburns
sweep the sidewalks in smiling rows.
They wear each other's clothes
by way of compliment, exchange toupees

at noon under the boom of the burgherly clock.
A precarious satisfaction trickles
from their mouths, no greater than my own.

And on the south side, they say,
some have never seen the lake.
Whole educational systems have been devised
and cafeteria programs. Secretaries of awareness
in pointed sweaters
continuously patrol the boundaries
of their concrete smile, whispering,
Forget, the lake is beside you.
The disbelievers hug themselves with powerful arms
in the back rows
and dream of wrenches and good bosoms.

All over the city, the congregation of the buses
shifts, again. The intoning of advertisements
goes on silently around us,
easing the strangling of the shopping bags.
A man gets on and sits in front of me
wearing a wad of chewing gum in the middle
of his back. I think of saving him
for a moment, but he saves himself
by getting up and leaving, by walking through you
with chewing gum stuck to the middle of his back.
What have you done with him?
Whose mark was he wearing?

But like this letter you are thinking of other things.
You want to go bowling or to your sister Rita's.
That is the nice thing about poets. You can go
to your sister Rita's and they will wait outside.
They will fetch beer if you run out
and stand in the dark counting telephone poles
until you are ready to go.

And all that time the conversation continues,
and when you pick it up four hours later
we are in the middle of the same word.

The empty stapler, the unsharpened pencil,
the dry rubberstamp of a dead executive,
instructions for the care of lenses,
the closed pipe-case, recipes for soap,
unanswered letters from Puerto Rico,
back issues still in plain brown wrappers,
bookmarks stuck into slanted texts
like flags in the sides of whales
hunted by other men in another time.

Today, I walked past the Hong Fat Co.
To have walked past the Hong Fat Co.
alone, the sun shining, and snow drifted
into the doorways of the bars across the street,
speaks for itself. Later, I walked up the hill
past the brewery where the old brick mansions
lie boarded and painted,
houses full of gothic cement,
mausoleums for the barons who built them
each with an owner cemented into bed.

But this is no time to speak of mausoleums.
A small worm has entered your skin
through the inhaling of its pores
and swum its way to your heart
where it fills your blood like an ocean
with infinite black sperm.
The gardens of your ocean luxuriate.
The underwater movement of slow bodies,
the underwater speech, the beat of your own heart
comes back, floating on slow sperm.

You think you are poisoned and about to die,
but that is your last heart beating back.

I like it when the beautiful young Negresses
climb aboard you like a public convenience
and use you. And the gray undergraduates
sit on the stairways of glass and memorize
levels of communication. Interpersonal,
they shout through the legs of ascending professors.
Intrapersonal. And someone memorizes his name.

Some would call this fallacy pathetic.
But I do not expect you to listen to me
except in the way you might listen
to traffic at the bottom of the afternoon,
the trembling of the windowpanes,
the conversation in the next life like water
running through the walls, leaves brushing.
The bush spoke to Moses because it had to.

The eastside mansions preen against their flags.
At night the snow blows through the spotlights
on its way to the flags and lifts up the skirts
of the twinkled Christmas frontlawn everywhere
wedding of the arctic pole. It's so difficult
to be wealthy, so responsible, so wise.
And you do not seem to mind. At night
I walk through your orange windows and count
the leathered bookbacks, touch your blue wallpapers,
swoon for the corners of your perfect paintings.
One night I saw the eldest son in the living room.
He pushed plants into the windows, threw incense
over the piano, took off his clothes and wept.
I stood a while and heard this weeping.
It was full of socialism and the three bears

to whom he promised more porridge in the morning
if they would vote for him, only vote for him.
The bears, whom I could not see,
demanded more porridge, more than porridge,
porridge now. Which, when they got, promptly
put them into a deep sleep from which
it is said they will hardly ever wake.
And on the lawns they are whistling Dixie.
And in the homes they are coaxing children
into the world, pounding their mitts of stone
and singing, "hum babe, hum that pea."

Let your houses come down.
Let them feel the bite of the crane.
Let their intimacies come into the open,
their pale stains flowering the rubble.
Let the students watch on their way to class.
When you put the grass back, unroll it slowly.
Or better yet, let it come back by itself.
The silence of the prairie's vengeance,
the squeak of the ungreased grassblade,
here where it is buried, would help us.
Let there be a vacant lot in our neighborhood
with broken bricks bulldozed into a cellarhole,
a place for children to make us
and stone us in the open air.

In a room beneath some of your rubble,
in an area patrolled by the wink of icepicks,
an escaped convict reads his confessions in the dark.
He confesses to everything,
all of it scrawled uphill in pencil
on bits of torn paper, stuffed in a gym-bag.
The whisper of thumbs alphabetizing
rises on featherless wings.

Nostalgia precedes my knowledge of you,
as it does of everything. Today,
in a photograph, I see my mother
for the first time, the new mother, the girl
just gone, stunned by the theft, the thief
grinning wickedly, the blob propped up
by an outspread hand, wider than memory,
furrowed with blood and the hint
of women harnessed to a dead stick
at the back of winter. And over it all,
the slack-clothed sag of the immigrant.
I see now why I am here
writing these letters to no one
in a language no one speaks.

Daily, I let poems slide past me.
I see them coming and I think of arranging
the glot of grief in my throat
and the whole exhalation machine,
but when they come, I let them go.
It must mean something to have
so many poems in one place
and to feel like leaving them where they are.
It is like the sacred cow of India
who needs no invitation, who is worshipped
by being left alone.

NOW

Now, and in the face of all bearable
obstacle and impediment, and without
benefit of sanctifying or
otherwise corroborating theory
or device, free of all haunting visions
and insecurities of mind, open
as much to the spider's drool as to
the implacable stone and shadowed marvel
of the hours, in full cognizance and reach
of the huge black wind blowing through our bones,
the needled sperm lash and the pus-born wish,
with throat extended and deep hypnotic hum
as of armies swarming, in daylight born
and in the darkness born once more, alone
but with those I love now close about me,
I, Roger, abstract speck upon the void,
reeking with wild and half immaculate
satisfaction, do hereby state and make,
in the numbed presence of my enemies,
the worm, the laundry, and the arch-fiend greed,
a cloak of pure conflicting rhetorics,
a gaudy panoply of smirks, a yip,
that that indifferent brute boo-ha in me
should not go naked or, what's worse, unseen.

THE LITTLE TABLE

I don't know where to begin this poem.
I don't know what to make it say.
I am not worrying, for the moment,
about the number of syllables in the line.
There are as many syllables as there are.
I will not refuse to admit any of them.
The least of them may be the key,
the most inconsequential and expendable article.
I am alone with my language,
the whole of it. It begs me to say
the simplest and most difficult things,
without intervention, without artifice.
When I tell it that it will not live forever that way,
it has a fit in the hallway.
It breaks the little table there, the one
that seems to have no function and is brown.
I do not know what you call it. It is very little.
And now it is broken.

RELATIONS

Impossible to erect some refuge
of intellect or wit, better to stick
my neck in a yoke I know and drag it
in that direction, the bright day bursting
with drops, the windows streaked.

I plunge into the relationless day,
licking its long sides, feeling its edges.
The postmaster's wife who gave me the wrong change,
the gravelled lane, the short-skirted woman
lugging rug samples into the suburbs,
or whatever this ring of new houses is,
the woman singing her daughter to school,
smoothing the way for a long separation.

Last night I drove to a pub in the next
village, sat there a stump in the low room,
drank my pint and drove off singing the blues
into the twisted, hedge-pinched lanes, some tune thumped
out of the juke box in my brain. "Daddy,
where do you get all those songs," asked Molly
one night. When I'm alone, I sing. Sometimes
I wash the dishes. The year in Poland
it was shoes. I polished my shoes daily,
listened to Radio Peking and drank
vodka, czysty, and good Georgian cognac,
sure that I was helping end the cold war.

That's what I wanted then, and I had means,
so I thought, small means. Ignorant good will
and a faith in reason. Reason given
a shove perhaps, like Martin Luther King,
but reason nevertheless. Now reason

seems to have left us. And into its hole
we stuff ourselves, gorged on fantasies
of power, criminal and sexual,
political, and even, sometimes,
the completely gratuitous, the bash.
Or the dissembled disinterest in it,
the hip disaffection, the slipped eyelid,
the limp nod of the assenting junkie.
Reason's departure seems to have left us
the real reason, which we recoil from
as if stung, or put to our own uses.
That right should be done because it is right
becomes a primitive way of thinking,
still to be hoped for, but useless to those
who still suffer because it is not done.

In today's paper — I almost forgot —
the beautiful face of Hortense Allende
whose "almost inaudible Spanish" breaks
two years of silence for the murdered right.

IN THE HOWARD JOHNSON'S IN HAMMOND

In the Howard Johnson's in Hammond
the waitress asks me where I am going.
She smiles as though she were Kay Leech
and it was 1951 and Saranac Lake
had just tied Malone and nothing,
not anything, had ever happened.
As though I were walking back in moonlight,
miles and miles in thick moonlight,
having said goodnight to a girl whose name
I am trying to remember, a girl I thought
would never speak to me, whom I think kissed me
on the back steps, near the end of summer,
on the outskirts of Lake Placid in 1953,
though I am still not sure, and have forgotten
what I must have felt, then, I could not forget.
She stands at the back door in moonlight
and I'm sure, almost positive, says "Thank you
for walking me all the way," and kisses me
and goes indoors. It was miles,
and the moonlight never stopped coming,
and I never went back and I can't think, still,
of her name, or why I never went back,
though I'm sure she kissed me, a touch
on the lips. I could take you there now,
I could show you the green farmhouse,
the plain wooden building. I could show you
the back step, the blurred light in a boy's chest.
Except that I'm going the other way.

Whoever you were, wherever you are,
spirit alive in me yet, I wait by the door
of the Howard Johnson's in Hammond
to say, when she comes back from the kitchen,
"Good Luck," as I go where I'm going.

56

WHO NEEDS A BICYCLE

> *An artist needs Marx like a fish needs a*
> *bicycle*
>
> — *Hank Malone*

A fish needs a bicycle like
a worm. The worm needs a new coat.
It is not for me to say no
to the fish's or the worm's wants.
Each has its separate color
and consistency, its own glow.
Each wants more than it has or is
and may be entitled to most
or all of it, subject to need.
If you find this fantastic, think.

I think of the discontented
fish flinging itself at the sand
for a long time. Until it walked,
in fact, on a kind of stiffened
fin, or limped. Into, let us say,
a mouth, thinking, This is the way
to the bicycles. In the mouth
there it met other eaten things
also looking for bicycles.
They sat down and sang this song: We
are the fish come out of the sea.

THE CHOICE

The choice I had then was the choice I had,
and I saw it, mostly, and I chose well,
falling, as I knew I would then, though not
in any of the ways I then foresaw.

Naturally, I chose the repressive way,
having been sat on with love from the womb
on, fighting the love I needed with rage
that I could not win what I did not want.

When the bus left, I was not on it,
and it was not me who got thrown off
with puke caked in a beard I did not have
then, the stars barking in the desert dawn.

The other side of myself came to me
fitfully, chiselling the thick structures
I had been given, and clung to, adding,
where possible, fresh boulders to the dam.

I was a perfect product, at certain
moments or in particular, fleeting
slants of attitude and bearing. The light
had to be just right, though, and the crowd hushed.

Secretly, and with time less secretly,
I became, or since I already was,
I was willing to acknowledge myself,
even show myself, confused and ungood.

It hurt to be so mortal, and I strove
not to be. I mastered my feelings grimly
and cheered when they were thrown, my self-love saved.
At night my body lashed me with its dreams.

I look like anyone else in a crowd.
I still wear the khaki of my post-war youth.
Though I know better now what I'm doing,
I still do it. Truth has made me truthful

only. And since I can't, or won't, change,
I confess. Albeit in a language
muted with circumspection and clotted
with succulent bursts of complication.

UPRIGHT AND FALLEN

There is an impassive, stolid brutality
about the woods, that has never been
enough insisted on.
— *Charles Dudley Warner*

The featureless bland faces of Homer's boy hunters, impassive
as in watching with equanimity and disinterest the work
of their own hands, the log laid low or the hand-made knife
as its blade passes in gray light under the terrified throat,
stolid as in doing the thing doggedly, as in thinking this
is the only way, the boy-like innocence of the boy, foot cocked
on the stump, the dogs baying at the hide draped easily
over the barrel of the rifle which itself rides loosely
across the shoulder of the boy who gazes, or if not gazes,
lifts his face into the air, glazed with sunshine and sweat.

So that, without moving, as though by trick of the eye,
the boy joins the things he stands among, disappearing
among the leaping and draped forms, the upright and fallen,
blood-spattered browns, mud-shaped swales, glint and froth.
It is all one and sundered, and nothing comes back whole
but comes, if at all, like the fawn seen nibbling, quickly,
or the child full of distance it still hasn't travelled.
The gentlest wrist, blood threading its bones, is cruel,
the tree standing there and the weeds looking for light.
I have hated a stone for being there, for being a stone.

A CLEAR SPACE

I write all this from England.
It is raining. A blackbird stands
under a bush. The wind blows.
It is cold and I'm home alone,
or in this room which, for a while,
passes for home. I count the days.
The news from home is spotty, holes
in silence. Friends sicken or fall
away from each other. Someone
has moved. Another left. Another,
who was once close, answers the mail
infrequently. Whatever brought us
together weakens like stone walls,
which the local version of hoods
pulls apart in the dark. Time hums
and I hum with it, remembering
friends from the past, wishing we lived
in a way that kept us together.
My daughters rush into the room,
crying "Milwaukee, Milwaukee,"
loud with the wounds of their wrenching.
Difficult not to imagine
oneself doing the thing alone,
stripping as if for a deep plunge
in a frozen ocean, eyes shut.
The boy who brings us our paper
is just that. He carries a life
in his pocket. The man standing
at the plant gate, dwarfed by the "I"
of MOBIL in East Chicago,
was that John Eubanks? The waitress
is somebody's daughter. Faces
I see seem like faces I've seen,
until the place I inhabit

seems almost the world, where things
fall apart, but for good reason,
and nothing outlasts its use,
where even affection wears down,
and, like it or not, I sit here
in a clear space on a cold day
and look through my life to see it.

FOR THE CHILDREN AT U.S. GRANT SCHOOL, SHEBOYGAN, WISCONSIN

I remember hearing my mother cry.
It wasn't much more than a small sob
like a cat rolling over and stretching
or a hinge on a dry day or table leg dragged.
But I didn't know mothers cried, then.
It was something babies did. Or sissies.
I must have thought that when you grew up
everything was all right, that you were fixed,
at last, like a clock or a pair of skis.
It was when I heard my mother cry,
from another room, through a closed door,
that I began to wonder.
                              I began to wonder
what else I didn't know that I thought I knew.
Did everything keep secrets? The snow.
Did it fall only to rise again?
Was that the tree talking back when you stepped on the stair?
Or was hair a kind of water that your hands drank?

On the day that my mother tried to hide
her feelings, she gave me mine.

OF WILLIAM STILLMAN (1828-1901)

His life lived in the semi-pathetic way
of the post-Romantic man of leisure,
his genius dispersed, ambition blunted,
by too close a glimpse of something,
   which I will get to.

Later, travelled, did jobwork for newspapers,
the government, consul in a few places,
called himself finally a journalist,
who had it in him to paint, and did,
   briefly.

One hangs in the Concord Public Library
which I have seen only in bad reductions,
black and gray, in books, not about him,
but Emerson, who stands mute in the middle of it,
   looking lost and away.

Not that he gave up art. Who wouldn't have then?
Most lit out for Europe at the first chance
or locked themselves up at home, did not come back
or out, the work assuming that flow and stoppage,
   like wrapped feet

among Chinese nobility, a badge of enviable
uselessness. Stillman, though, is useful now,
so far from the nineteenth century and the thing
he saw there which many, even the brightest,
   neglected to mention

or carried like a last meal into the ground,
bits of half-digested organic matter,
we're not sure what, maybe corn meal and water.

I speak of the woods partly,
          partly of something else.

Certainly not that clump at the edge of town
or the next county, where one picnics among barrels
full of aluminum cans, but the thing that vanished
about the same time, and for most of the same reasons
          as the Indian.

We have here in Indiana a patch, I have seen it,
of uncut trees, original growth. An acre or two, at best.
People drive for miles just to look at it.
Whole families, if large enough, can hug
          its biggest tree.

It is a zoo to us, a kind of gorilla
brought from another continent, as bananas are brought
to the supermarket, an invisible miracle,
as in stooping to pick up a tossed bottle we forget
          we are stooping.

Stillman went there in '54 and found what he knew
his going there would kill. "This superb solitude,"
Emerson called it in his two-week camp-out four years later
with Agassiz and the rest, each with a guide,
          Stillman the host,

who stayed on after the others left,
sent his guide back to the settlement,
one of the Martins, I think, from Saranac,
and didn't come out till November,
          and nearly not then.

The wilderness dwindles (is gone, really)
under the human needs for it, Stillman

one of the last to feel there, as if by reversion,
the hush of creation, world before man.
            Which is why

this man, an American, at his life's end,
tried to make in the blunt soil of Frimley Green, Surrey,
his home of the moment, with cuttings and seeds
sent there from Albany, a thing that was now only
            inside him.

THE TWO SECRETARIES

Yesterday, I was distracted by the waiter.
You had just said something about men
and first marriages when he stuck his arm
between us. He stuck his arm between us
several times. Thick plates clattered in back of us.
It was that part of the restaurant
and that part of the day. I said nothing then
of the two young women sitting next to us,
the one on my side closer to me than you.
Though it was secretly their conversation
I was listening to. No one could have guessed.
Not even you, who have had to put up with
my faulty attention longer than you'd like to.
They talked about Jews and Catholics.
They talked about Protestants. They were wondering
who was what at the office, and why.
"If you're not Jewish or Catholic," said the one
closer to you, the one whose face I avoided
looking into, "you must be Protestant."

The cracked plate shone under the cannelloni.
It was their own world they were digging up,
bits of it glinted with thought.
One of them was Black, so I thought of my daughters.
"I think of you every day," I told them
in the second year of the divorce. I hoped,
I suppose, that thinking might keep them from harm
or the dozen small things this side of harm.

Let me say this once, and then be done with it.
The day I drove them away, Molly was still.
I could hear the pistons thumping in the block.
Bridget broke into sobs that she couldn't stop.
I had driven their mother to the edge of town

months before and left her next to a truck,
a U-Haul truck with a bright wide band around,
and in it the nicked chairs and the sad bed.
I think we shook hands. We may have said thanks,
or good luck.

I think of them not many years from now,
saying to someone somewhere in a sure voice,
"Catholics go to mass" or "Jews are not
Protestants," putting the ruin together
again, most of which I have forgotten
to tell them about, though not all. And so,
have added to their innocence and,
I can almost believe, to the gradual
elimination of the past, the best of the past,
I realize, but also the worst.

What we did with the rest of that day tumbles
into memory, though I think it was then
that we stood before Titian's "Man in a Red Cap,"
at Seventieth and Fifth Avenue.
Whose slightly flared hair and vulnerable lean
toward the frame, exciting the English ladies
behind us, told us in twenty seconds or so
why that merchant democracy, once Othello's,
could not bear the weight of itself, but fell
into the mazy streets and clean stones
we went half way round the world to see.

MAMOO' S DEATH

Molly says she remembers. I wonder.
I've mentioned the trip often enough,
so often she may remember only
my asking. It's strange what family means,
how much and how little, like a first kiss.
Does anyone remember farther back
than a stray great grandmother or so?
We don't seem built to carry more than that.
The others fall off the edge. The world
is never more than a hundred years old.
And that only because some old woman
sits in a corner and tells stories
the dead can't quarrel with. History is who lasts.
People turn into gestures or phrases
or something done once in anger or love.
For a while, anyway.
                                You seemed to know that.
Which of your stories will I tell the most,
who have already begun to lose your face?
I can't get the last one out of my head.
You entering the oven on a plain tray,
having said, "When you're through, throw me away."

SEEING ENGLAND

How totally everything's changed,
and how little it seems to matter.
I can see where the hedgerows were,
a strip in the field with a tree
or two along it where the hay
sputters or refuses to grow.
The garden's a car park now. Shops
in the village dwindle to knick-
knacks and gifts as the chains collect
in the neighboring towns. Neighbors
are strangers in a new way now,
will soon be mugging each other.
Occasional graces display
themselves, habits of speech, a pint
bought for the senile pensioner,
the willow preserved on the lawn
of the new semi-detached home,
a limp reminder of water
and cows that grazed in the front room,
a horseshoe found in the garden.

Whatever this place was to me
when I first came to it is gone.
Most of what it was in my head
before, of course, was never there.
Like Eliot in Russell Square.
I stood there on my first morning,
just after dawn, thinking he might
drive up and read me a poem
or tell me to drop in for tea.
We walked all week, propping ourselves
up with history, a living book.
The bomb craters made us wonder,

perilously near the real thing.
We stared into one or two holes
dumbly, imagining life there.

For us England was like a toy,
one that had all the parts, in scale,
where tiny sheep cropped tiny fields,
the trains really worked, the beer fizzed,
the streets had curbs, like the feelings,
the eyes closed when you laid them down.
A brightly painted collection
of quaint customs, impartial laws,
that one could take out and play with
like a memory of childhood,
the occasionally chipped paint
being part of the quaintness,
part of our hope that, like Pepsi,
we needn't happen to everything.

We haven't, of course. And we won't.
In the meantime a pallor falls
on everything, even England.
Through which we see, more easily,
real people doing real things.

SOME THING

Does not seem like enough to have
reached forty and be about to
make a big wisdom with the mouth.
Right now I want to know something.
Not something about something but
some thing, the lot, I want to know
how many hairs grow on my head,
exactly, or better yet, who
had the most to eat yesterday.
I want to know why BIC pens cost
less in England, or if they do.
I want to know what they're made of,
down to the tiny ink-soaked ball,
and where they get what it's made of,
and for what wages, and what's left
after the loggers or the drillers
(or whoever they are) chop down
the pink-veined forests of plastic,
and what's left after the wages
have done what they have to do. What
is this world I live on top of?
I want to know why I should have
to want to know. It is not clear.
Have I kept myself ignorant,
studying for these twenty years?
Have I not ever needed to know?
What is the consequence of this,
or the cause? The darkness is fine,
but finally it is just dark.
One moves so gracefully in it,
or can, the stumbling is taken
for honesty. Or, a new move.

STARTING TO STARVE

There are fewer people, I notice,
everywhere. There are fewer
people at the baseball games.
There are fewer people dying.
At the sign of the abandoned
gas station, a few people stand
in line, a few hunker down.

A few of my friends are gone, one
never finished his training, drifted
from one bad job to another,
thinking he might, if he found a reason,
disappeared from sight in my own
city, though I may have waved to him
once, came back at a party.

In name only. Someone had seen him.
I remember a party at his
apartment. There were lots of people
there. Now he's run out of jobs,
even the bad ones, is starting
to starve, as he says, or I heard
he said, as a few people are.

I try to imagine the moment
when you start to starve, the first time
you finish and still want more,
the first time you lick the plate.
Or is it the first time you pay
more than you ought to for something
you need, or start eating beans

all the time. Yes, they would laugh
at this poem in Africa. They would
probably not read it. They would
probably never see it, or if,
by mistake, it came there, this year,
wedged among leaflets and wheatseed,
they would probably eat it.

THE STORY OF THE WHITE CUP

for Helen

I am not sure why I want to tell it,
since the cup was not mine, and I was not there,
and it may not have been white, after all.
When I tell it, though, it is white, and the girl
to whom it has just been given, by her mother,
is eight. She is holding a white cup against her breast,
and her mother has just said good bye, though those
could not have been, exactly, the words. No one knows
what her father has said, but when I tell it,
he is either helping someone very old with a bag
or asking a guard for a cigarette. There is, of course,
no cigarette. The box cars stand with their doors
slid back. They are black inside, and the girl
who has just been given a cup and told to walk
in a straight line and to look like she wants
a drink of water, who cried in the truck
all the way to the station, who knew, at eight,
where she was going, is holding a cup to her breast
and walking away, going nowhere, for water.
She does not turn, but when she has found water,
which she does, in all versions of the story, everywhere,
she takes a small sip of it and swallows.

VISITING COUNTRY GRAVES
WITH MY DAUGHTERS

We are figuring out what happens, here,
in a small space pushed out among trees.
It is the second day of three, and we
know it. Even plastic flowers fade.
The dye won't hold. Nor will they stay in place,
blown or possibly flung into the weeds.
Out of the woods a warble comes. The weeds
will last forever. The limestone plinths perch
on the edge of something blank. If we stayed,
we could find out what. But the day wavers.
Tomorrow is the third of three, and we
must sleep and rise into its outstretched arms.
One more stone before we go. We drift
apart, calling the names of strangers, back
and forth, the day they came, the day they left.

KEENE VALLEY, LATE FALL, STARSET

Standing in the meadow above the rush of the unseen river,
dusk, and the air gray along the edges of the west mountains,
the leaves half fallen and the rest turned yellow-brown,
the air cool and getting cooler quickly, the sky clear,
clear the way sky that has been clear all day is clear,
and the one star in the whole sky above the nearest mountain
setting, and trying to wish quickly, the way I was taught,
secretly, before the second star appears, before the blink,
standing in the open meadow, the huge house moored behind me,
its one light casting itself thinly across the grass,
across the now deserted garden scattered with compost and ash.
And not knowing, finally, what to wish for. And so
not wishing at all, but standing there watching a star move.

THE INCIDENT OF THE WATER

Clear water splashed on my folded pants,
not yet soaked in, still humped on the surface.
I tried sliding it off by lifting them.
Next, her hair and face appeared, also splashed.
I may have known for an instant who did it,
or what. I suppose it might have been me.
But I lost interest, hoping to save my pants,
wiping them, sliding the water off.

The water changed her. She became a dwarf.
I watched it happen, the skin going taut
across her forehead. I had never looked
closely at her. I knew what she looked like.
That was enough. We had held each other
as tenderly, I think, as people could.
I remember the cloudy feel of her skin.

But there was the incident of the water
and of the two of us looking at the other
while it was happening. We did nothing
but look. There was nothing we could do.
A clock had struck midnight somewhere,
or one of us had turned and looked at the other.
There had been some unforgivable breach.
We knew it at once, though not what or where.
It was too late to wish we had been warned.
Maybe we had been. It might have been the pants,
folded. It was useless to want the facts.
There may not have been any. She was gone,
and though I hung about, dazed, I was too.

THE HISTORY OF THE WIND

for Lisel Mueller

In the early days,
when there were no worlds
to brush against, no stars
to catch in the eye, the wind
had only itself to sing to,
a small tuneless hum.

There was wind,
and there was nothing.

And the wind stayed there,
which was everywhere,
for a long time, a princess
locked in an upper room
hoping that a prince might
pass by underneath.

She sang to catch his attention.

When we drifted by, at last,
neither a prince
nor very good looking,
she let down her song anyway,
long, complicated tresses,
thick, rivery braids.

This one seems nice enough, she said.
Who knows when the next one will come along.

She was with us the rest of our days,
even when she wasn't.
Even when she went out crazy,

driving the back roads.
Dry, motionless afternoons,
late rain, and humid nights.

We sat them out, mostly, fanning ourselves.

Older now, and more wise,
she sings when she wants to.
Like someone who has stopped caring
what others think of her,
she combs her hair when she feels like it
and spits at the neighbor boys
when they taunt her.

I'm not going to die, she says.
Not ever.